COLORS

words

ken.
nordine

pictures

henrik drescher

Library of Congress Cataloging-in-Publication Data
Colors/Ken Nordine; illustrated by Henrik Drescher.
p.   cm.
Summary: A collection of poems personifying fifteen different colors.
ISBN 0-15-201584-1
[1. American poetry. 2. Color—Poetry.] I. Drescher, Henrik. II. Title.
1. Juvenile poetry, American. 2. Color—Juvenile poetry.
PS3564.05612C65   2000
811'.54—dc21   97-23073

First edition
A C E F D B
Printed in Singapore

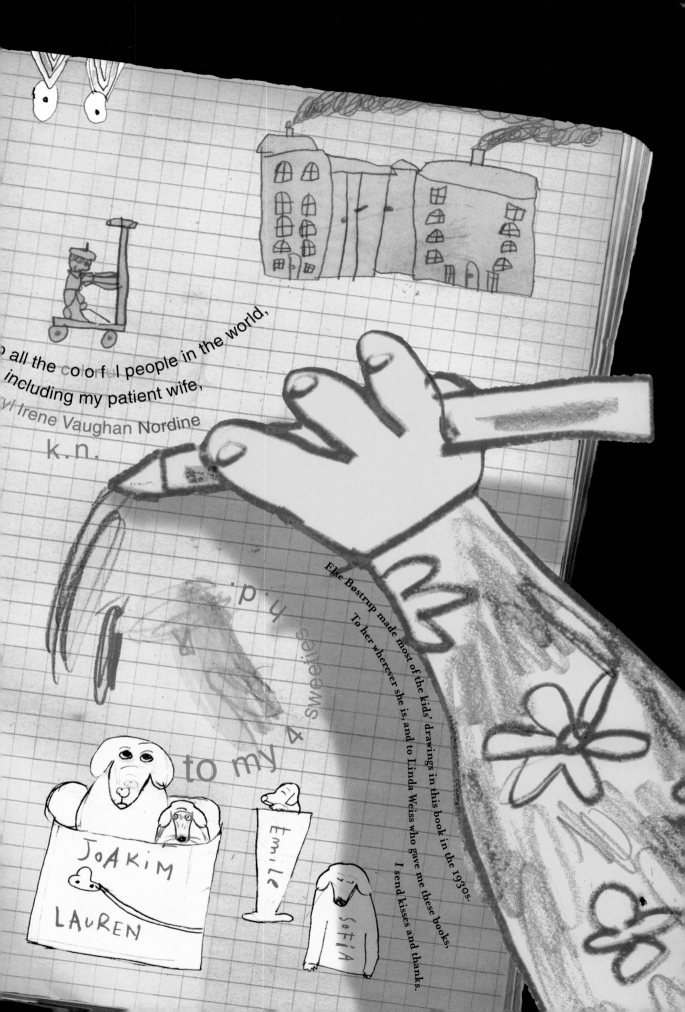

To all the colorful people in the world,
including my patient wife,
Irene Vaughan Nordine

k.n.

to my 4 sweeties

JOAKIM
LAUREN

Emile

SoFiA

Else Bostrup made most of the kids' drawings in this book in the 1930s.
To her wherever she is, and to Linda Weiss who gave me these books,
I send kisses and thanks.

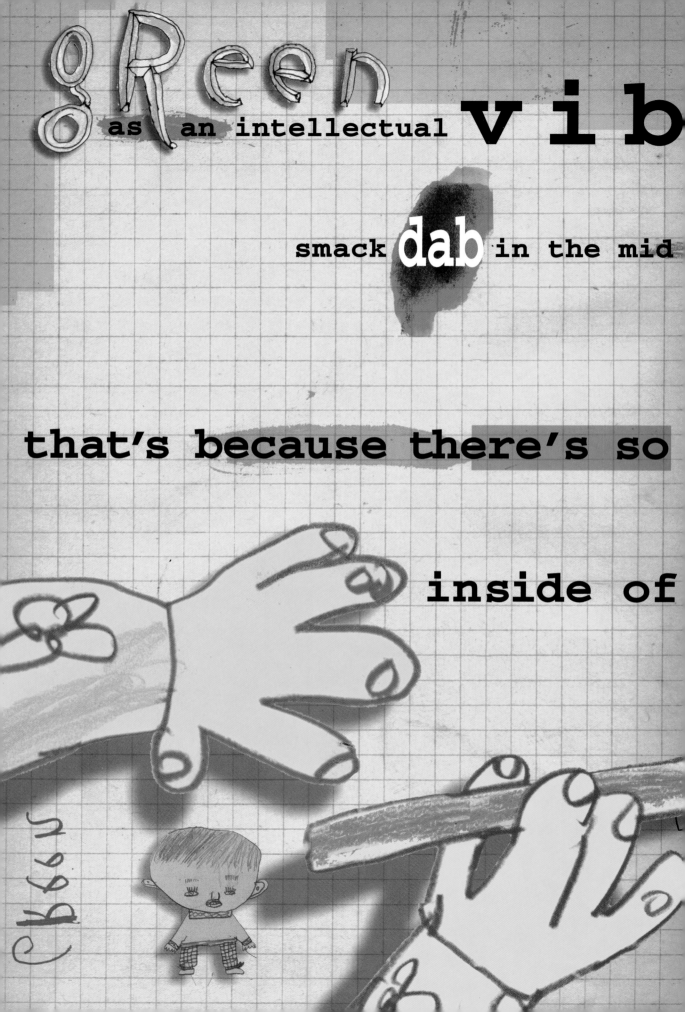

gReen as an intellectual vib

smack dab in the mid

that's because there's so

inside of

ration,

dle of spectrum,

can be a problem

many different greens

GREEN ...

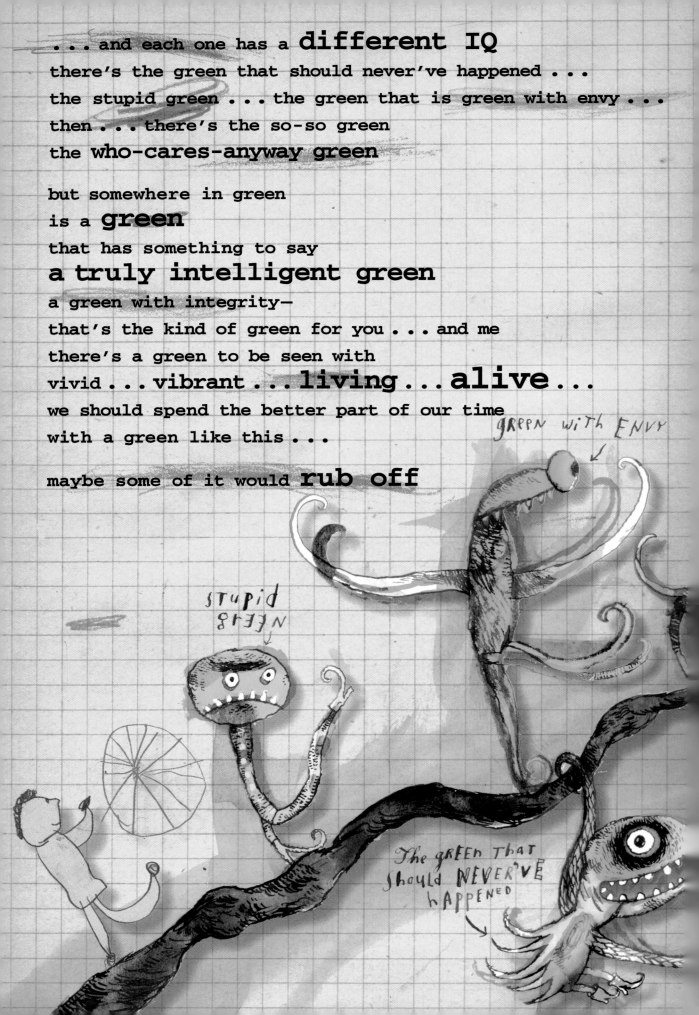

... and each one has a **different IQ**
there's the green that should never've happened ...
the stupid green ... the green that is green with envy ...
then ... there's the so-so green
the **who-cares-anyway green**

but somewhere in green
is a **green**
that has something to say
a truly intelligent green
a green with integrity—
that's the kind of green for you ... and me
there's a green to be seen with
vivid ... vibrant ... **living ... alive ...**
we should spend the better part of our time
with a green like this ...

maybe some of it would **rub off**

GREEN WITH ENVY

stupid
green

The GREEN THAT
should NEVER'VE
HAPPENED

SO-SO GREEN

who-CARES-Anyway GREEN

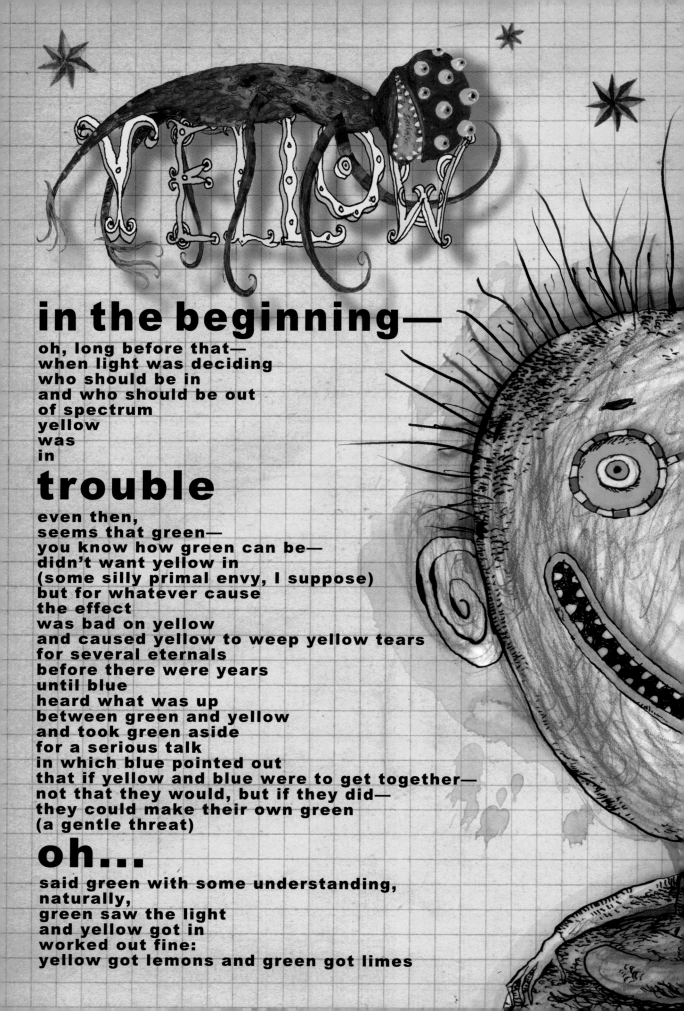

YELLOW

in the beginning—

oh, long before that—
when light was deciding
who should be in
and who should be out
of spectrum
yellow
was
in

trouble

even then,
seems that green—
you know how green can be—
didn't want yellow in
(some silly primal envy, I suppose)
but for whatever cause
the effect
was bad on yellow
and caused yellow to weep yellow tears
for several eternals
before there were years
until blue
heard what was up
between green and yellow
and took green aside
for a serious talk
in which blue pointed out
that if yellow and blue were to get together—
not that they would, but if they did—
they could make their own green
(a gentle threat)

oh...

said green with some understanding,
naturally,
green saw the light
and yellow got in
worked out fine:
yellow got lemons and green got limes

AZURE

as sure as there's azure it's sure to be true
azure is bored with just being blue
a fact that has caused our dear friend
to act sort of silly
like he's at his wit's end
azure's as way out as wink
maybe more out than that
a winkier wink
you'd never've guessed
but azure can think
of the craziest things to do
besides tinting the atmosphere's top, I mean
the part we all call sky blue,
azure would rather
so I've been told
let the sky be a white upside-down bowl
that azure could azure with clouds inside
or possibly freckle with birds...look...
if azure could read
or write in a book
it would want every thought
it could azurely think
to be written in azure
with azure ink

why?

just to be different
that's the name of the game
you see, azure can't stand
being anything same

BLACK

as the ace of spades is

BLACK

as a hole in Calcutta is

BLACK

as a jack in the game is

BLACK

as my true love's hair is

BLACK

as a dreamless sleep is

BLACK

as a midnight is

as closing your eyes tight is

as a little black sheep is...

BLACK

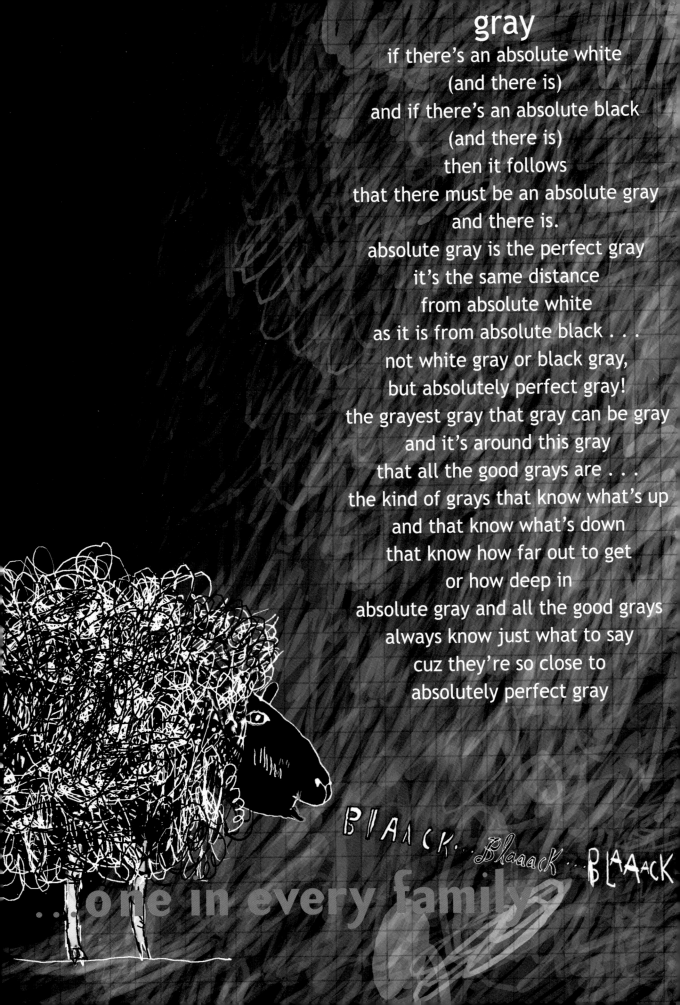

gray

if there's an absolute white
(and there is)
and if there's an absolute black
(and there is)
then it follows
that there must be an absolute gray
and there is.
absolute gray is the perfect gray
it's the same distance
from absolute white
as it is from absolute black . . .
not white gray or black gray,
but absolutely perfect gray!
the grayest gray that gray can be gray
and it's around this gray
that all the good grays are . . .
the kind of grays that know what's up
and that know what's down
that know how far out to get
or how deep in
absolute gray and all the good grays
always know just what to say
cuz they're so close to
absolutely perfect gray

BIAACK . . . Blaaack . . . BIAAACK

. . .one in every family

white
take a close look
yeah...
but much closer than that
take a real close look
you begin to see why
there's much more to white
much more
than can ever fill the eye
like...look over there...
there!
you see that white?
sure looks for sure
like the white that's called pure
but it isn't
not at all
that's an off-white white
sorry
just doesn't quite measure up
falls short
absolutely pure pure white
is a dream of a dream

even now
if you close your eyes tight
and let your brain go
to where it's whiter than snow
you'll see...you'll know
that the whitest white
that white can be white
as imagined by you
imagined by me
as the purest of pure pure white
is just a little bit off...
just a little bit off...white...
off-white white...off-white white

BLAAACK...BLAACK

LAVENDER

lavender
is an old old old old lady
lavender is
aren't you?
I thought you were
lady lavender in the indigo house
by the purple wood
cobwebbed by spiders
and magic magenta
lavender
keeper of dark corners
and black blue blood
lady of the soft edges
tell us all
or tell me
where day goes with night
and what they do there
and what it means
the questions fall on your lavender lap
and your answer is
a lavender laugh in a lavender cry
near a lavender what by a lavender why

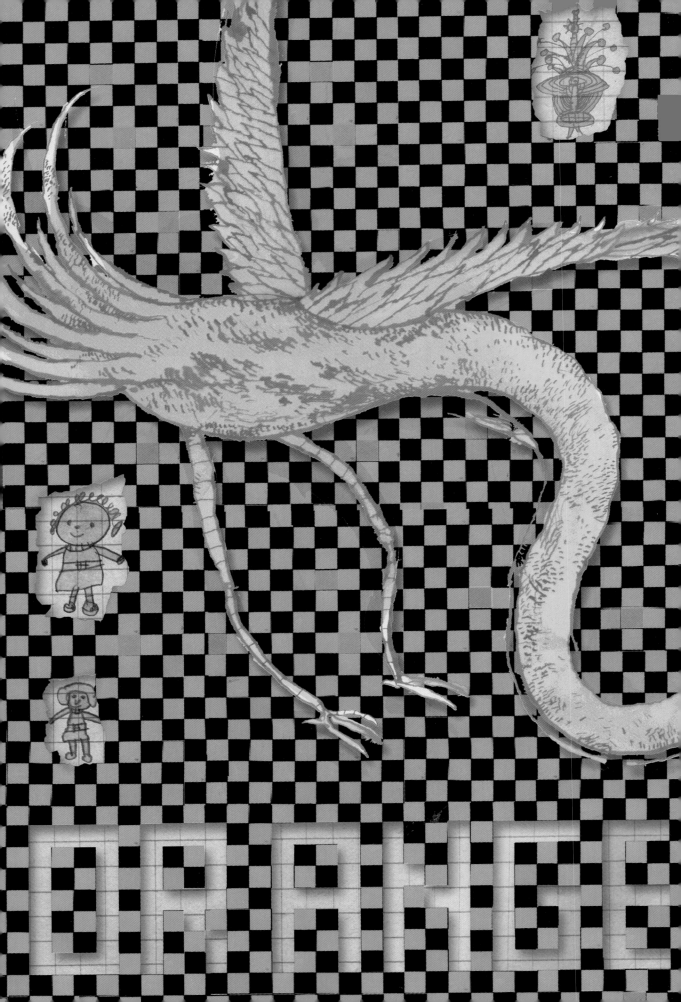

# of all the colors

under the sun
only one color I think is much fun
and that's orange.
orange, I said...
the silly old color
that lives next to red.
the one that is orangely out of its head...

that giggles and titters
and rolls in the aisle
no matter what happens
guffaws all the while,
old orange . . .
as flip as a high-spinning coin,
or a stone skipping watery skips

an orangey bird
with orangey wings
with orangey songs
that it orangely sings
that orangely comes
as it orangely goes
laughing in orange
from its head to its toes.
when everything's
orangey goofy like this

trouble's a joke—
just an orangey joke

only one trouble
troubles orange
if you please
that's in the morning . . .

it's the trouble called squeeze
changing orangey orange
into vitamin C's

yum!

chartreuse wanted to quit . . .
why not?
figured it would go off somewhere
be by itself
maybe let green or yellow take over
and get away from it all . . .
that's what chartreuse wanted . . .
who needs chameleons?
what difference would it make
in the immense design of things
if certain feathers were some other color?
parrots wouldn't care . . .
nor would parakeets . . .
but what about the leaves of rhubarb?

OOOOOooooohhhh..

chartreuse began to tremble
just thinking of the trouble rhubarb could make . . .
you know rhubarb
and the rhubarb that rhubarb could cause!
so chartreuse decided not to give notice
(not for a while anyway)
besides, isn't that a nervous katydid over there
that needs a new color?
of course!
chartreuse is gonna stay cuz it feels used

CHART REUSE

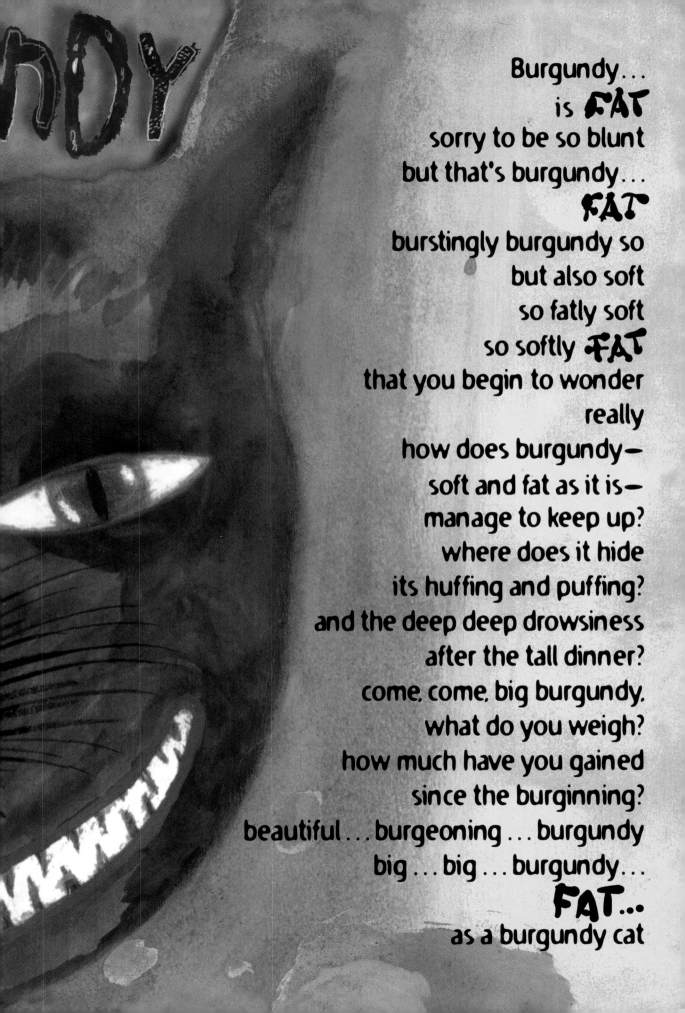

Burgundy...
is FAT
sorry to be so blunt
but that's burgundy...
FAT
burstingly burgundy so
but also soft
so fatly soft
so softly FAT
that you begin to wonder
really
how does burgundy—
soft and fat as it is—
manage to keep up?
where does it hide
its huffing and puffing?
and the deep deep drowsiness
after the tall dinner?
come, come, big burgundy,
what do you weigh?
how much have you gained
since the burginning?
beautiful ... burgeoning ... burgundy
big ... big ... burgundy...
FAT...
as a burgundy cat

FLESH, as a COLOR,

y e s !

ask anyone **with flesh! they'll tell you**

flesh, as a color,
is about as close to a problem
as a color can get
some people think
the only color flesh color should be
is the color their flesh color is
which
pure and simple
is colorcentric thinking
popular in some corners
but you and I know though
that the proper color for flesh to be
is the proper color it is
varying from complexion to complexion

but if black flesh
and white flesh
and brown flesh
and red flesh
and yellow flesh
and tan flesh

if all the fleshes that are flesh
want to establish a sensible sanity
among differences
we'd better forget the flesh
and the colors it can be
and think on the spirit and its singular light
otherwise
flesh, as a color,
could be black and blue

or even a bloody hue

PURPLE

all dignity...

ALL PoMP...

all put-on...
has an aura to be felt
as well as seen
purple has class
some say the highest
they stand in awe of purple
royally... loyally... in awe
this alone makes pompous purple king
king purple feels
there's a right that is his
that goes way back to the beginning
to the place where pomp began

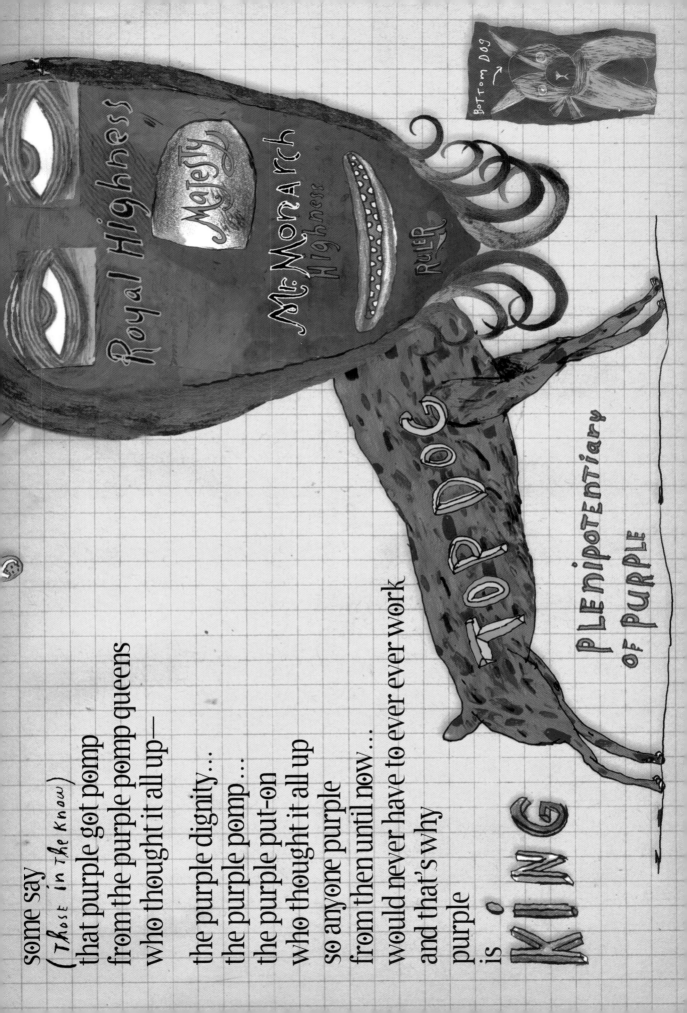

BOTTOM DOG →

Royal Highness

Majesty

Mr. Monarch
Highness

RULER

TOP DOG

KING

PLENIPOTENTIARY
OF PURPLE

some say
(Those in the know)
that purple got pomp
from the purple pomp queens
who thought it all up—

the purple dignity...
the purple pomp...
the purple put-on
who thought it all up
so anyone purple
from then until now...
would never have to ever ever work
and that's why
purple
is

olive, poor thing,
sits and thinks
that it's drab
sure does
sits and sits and sits and thinks

about its olive drab drab
doesn't know
that it is about to be named
color of the year
by those with a nose for the new
by the passionate few
yeah...
olive is definitely in
everything
that can possibly mean anything... **anywhere** (at least for a year)

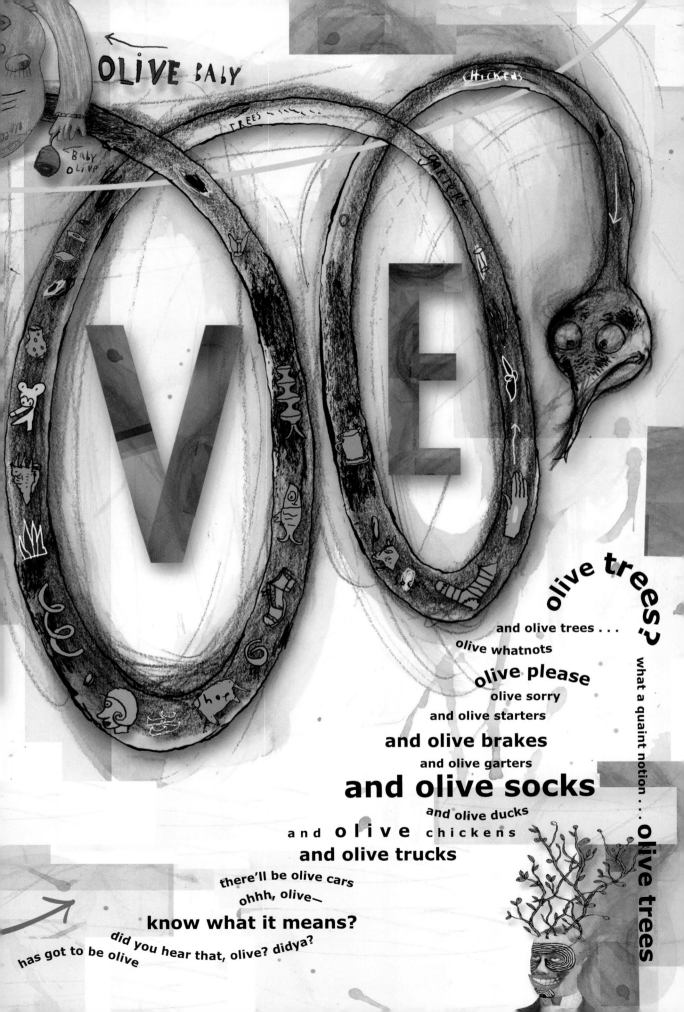

OLIVE BABY

← BABY OLIVE

V E

olive trees?

and olive trees . . .

olive whatnots

olive please

olive sorry

and olive starters

and olive brakes

and olive garters

and olive socks

and olive ducks

and olive chickens

and olive trucks

there'll be olive cars

ohhh, olive—

know what it means?

did you hear that, olive? didya?

has got to be olive

what a quaint notion . . . olive trees

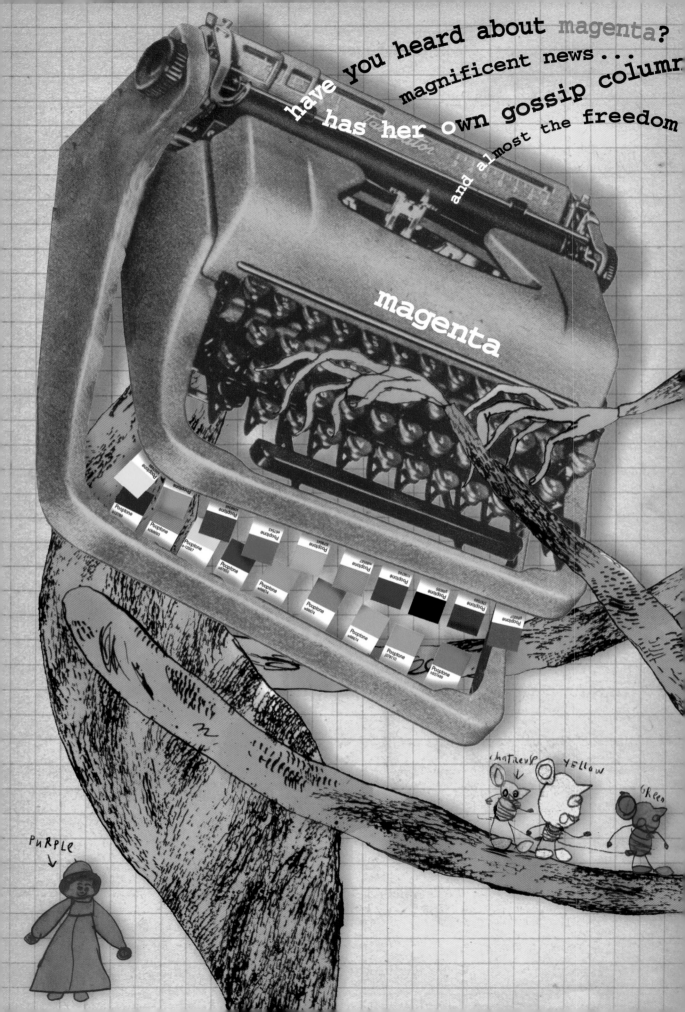

have you heard about magenta?
magnificent news...
has her own gossip column
and almost the freedom

magenta

CHaTReuse YELLOW GReen

PuRPLe

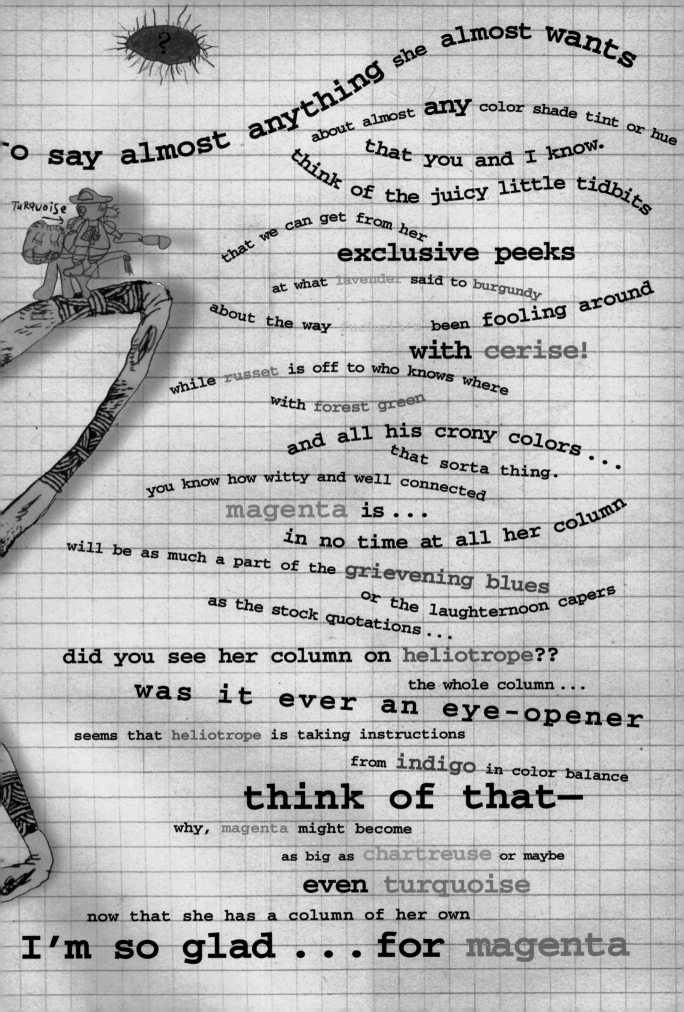

?

TURQUOISE

o say almost anything she almost wants

about almost any color shade tint or hue

that you and I know.

think of the juicy little tidbits

that we can get from her

exclusive peeks

at what lavender said to burgundy

about the way fuchsia's been fooling around

with cerise!

while russet is off to who knows where

with forest green

and all his crony colors...

that sorta thing.

you know how witty and well connected

magenta is...

in no time at all her column

will be as much a part of the grievening blues

or the laughternoon capers

as the stock quotations...

did you see her column on heliotrope??

was it ever an eye-opener

the whole column...

seems that heliotrope is taking instructions

from indigo in color balance

think of that—

why, magenta might become

as big as chartreuse or maybe

even turquoise

now that she has a column of her own

I'm so glad...for magenta

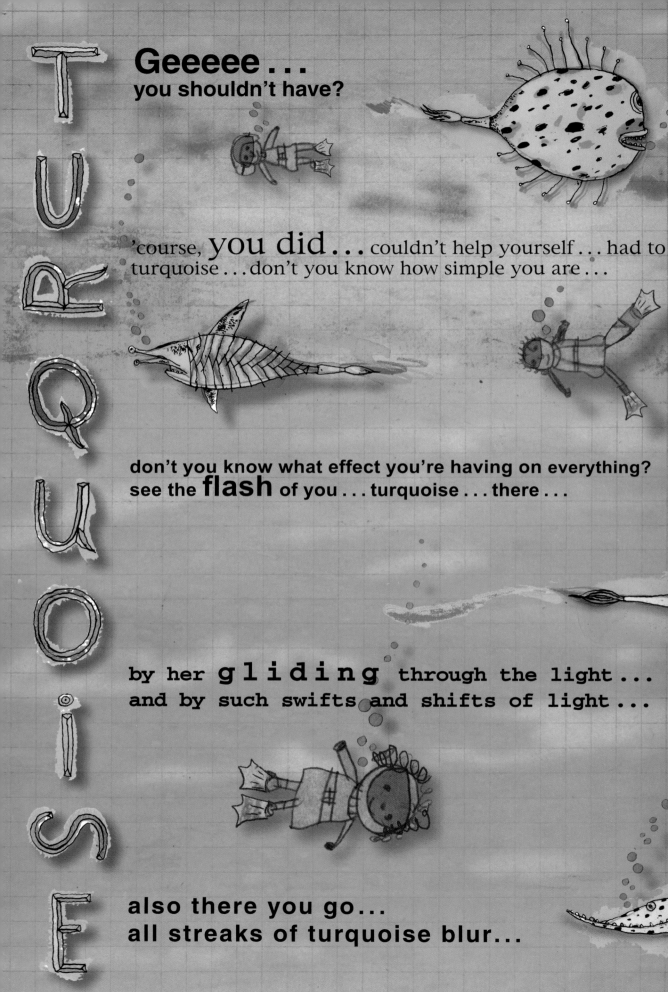

T U R Q U O I S E

Geeeee . . .
you shouldn't have?

'course, you did . . . couldn't help yourself . . . had to turquoise . . . don't you know how simple you are . . .

don't you know what effect you're having on everything? see the flash of you . . . turquoise . . . there . . .

by her **gliding** through the light . . .
and by such swifts and shifts of light . . .

also there you go...
all streaks of turquoise blur...

and here… **here**… a turquoise…
definitely so…

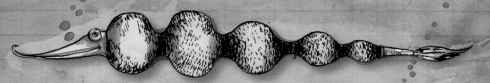

all tender… **t r e m b l i n g** like water
what do you think of a turquoise **like that?**

then…there's **this** turquoise…
and… **that** turquoise…

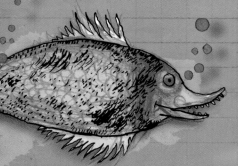

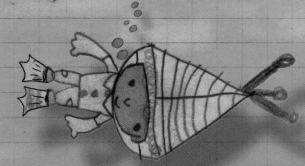

oh ho…turquoise…you shouldn't've…
'course, you did…couldn't help yourself

had to… isn't that right?
OH…

there's something…
that you can tint…
t u r q u o i s e